KAUA'I'S

NĀ PALI COAST

A UNIQUE ADVENTURE

PHOTOGRAPHY BY BRIAN MCDONALD • TEXT BY GRAHAM V. BELL
PRODUCED BY DOUG & BARBARA LUHMANN

UNIQUE ADVENTURES PRESS • SAN JUAN CAPISTRANO, CALIFORNIA

Photography and text copyright © 1990 by Unique Adventures Press
Photography by Brian McDonald
Text by GrahamV. Bell
Art Direction & Design by Barbara Luhmann
Produced by Doug and Barbara Luhmann

Printed in Hong Kong - Everbest Ltd.

ISBN 0-9627033-0-3

Unique Adventures Press
P.O. Box 185
San Juan Capistrano, California 92693

To our children, Emily, Blaine and Lolly
with all our love...

Doug and Barbara Luhmann

Contents

Preface: A Look Back at Ancient Hawaiian Social Structure

Introduction

Limahuli Valley/ National Tropical Botanical Garden

Kē'ē Beach

Hanakāpī'ai

Ho'olulu

Waiahuakua

Kalalau Beach

Kalalau Valley

Kalalau Beach to Hanakoa (including Pōhakuao)

Nākeikianā'i'iwi

Honopū

Awa'awapuhi

Nu'alolo

Miloli'i

Acknowledgements

Glossary

Bibliography

PREFACE: A LOOK BACK AT ANCIENT HAWAIIAN SOCIAL STRUCTURE

To better understand the myths and legends which are associated with the Nā Pali coast, we must first examine ancient Hawaiian social structure. Society was comparable to that of feudal Europe with the king, or *Ali'i Nui* at the top. The king's person was considered sacred, and he could not be looked upon by the commoners. The king's advisor was the *Kālaimoku*, or "island carver." One of his responsibilities was to divide the land up among the chiefs.

The land was divided up into *ahupua'a* and these were controlled by the chiefs, who were members of the "ali'i," or chiefly class. An ahupua'a was generally pie shaped, and since Kaua'i is almost round, its beginning point would have been in the center of the island. Each division had a mixture of forest, agricultural land, mountains and sea coast. The boundaries extended out into the ocean and included deep sea fishing rights and the right to harvest the bounty of the reefs. Ahupua'a because of their variety of terrain were self-sufficient. Each "ahupua'a" had a *"Konohiki,"* or lesser chief, and he also made sure that the land was cultivated, and that the *kapu* was enforced. Kapu were laws and restrictions governing different activities. There was even a kapu on fishing at certain times of the year. Kapu was the foundation of society, and when they were abandoned at the death of *Kamehameha I*, most of the old values were lost.

The *kāhuna* was not a class, but more the artisans. They were the master builders, the skilled navigators, the expert canoe builders, the priests, and the medicine men. Because they held positions of such power, they were second only to the ali'i.

The *"maka'āinana"* were the commoners and they could have no contact with the ali'i. If a commoner cast his shadow on an ali'i, he could be put to death. The "maka'āinana" were the fishermen, the farmers and the laborers. They were required to practice with their weapons, for in time of war the chief called upon them to serve as soldiers. Below them there was a class called the *"kauwā."*

The *"kauwā"* were the outcasts, and they had neither land nor rights. They were, perhaps, prisoners of war, or people who had lost their land because they had broken a kapu. They were basically slaves, and represented the lowest level of society. Some say they might have been the original inhabitants of the islands, the *Mu* people or the *Menehune*.

The most popular belief regarding the Menehune is that they were elf-like people with strong arms and legs. They were said to have been prodigious builders, who only worked at night. Some of their engineering feats included the Menehune ditch, which is an irrigation ditch, and the Menehune fish pond. There is a more plausible theory, which is neither as popular, nor as colorful.

In 1825, when a census was taken on Kaua'i, several Menehune were counted. This perhaps lends more credence to the theory that they were the original inhabitants.

"Manahune" has been the name that the Tahitians had used proudly to describe themselves. However, when they were conquered by the people of *Raiatea,* (a small island in the Tahitian archipelago) the term "Manahune" was used to describe people of the lower class. When the Tahitians came to Kaua'i, they did the same to the original inhabitants. Menehune is possibly a corruption of "Manahune," and instead of signifying small physical stature, it could have meant small social structure. This theory is very plausible, and is expressed by Edward Joesting in his book "Kaua'i, The Separate Kingdom."

INTRODUCTION

We invite you on a photographic journey of beauty and adventure as we tour the north west coast of Kaua'i. Here you will find 15 miles of rugged and magnificent scenery known as the Nā Pali coast, which is only accessible by boat, helicopter or the Kalalau trail.

Join us as we discover the gentle white beaches and tranquil shores of summer whose abundant treasures beckon beachcombers; the many sea caves whose mysteries add adventure for the daring traveler; and the raging surfs of winter which crash against the towering black lava cliffs. Inland on the trail you will find hanging valleys with ancient terraces in which cultivated *taro* patches grow among the gnarled *kukui* trees; where tumbling streams form magnificent waterfalls and cascade 3000 feet over the cliffs to the ocean below.

Come with us now, as we travel along the Nā Pali coast, sharing with you its picturesque beauty and describing its ancient myths and legends.

Limahuli Valley with Ha'ena State Beach in the foreground.
To the right of the valley is Makana Point, the beginning of
the Nā Pali coast.

LIMAHULI VALLEY

Mr. Charles "Chipper" Wichman, Jr., Superintendent-Horticulturist, of the Limahuli Gardens, Ha'ena.

Leaving our base in Princeville, we drove the short distance down highway 560 to the Ha'ena area, to keep our appointment with Charles Wichman, Jr., Superintendent-Horticulturist at the National Tropical Botanical Garden's satellite in the Limahuli Valley. Limahuli is not considered part of the Nā Pali coast, but much of Nā Pali's history, legends and plant life have ties with this valley, so it was a natural starting point for our tour. Charles Wichman was a wonderful source of information, and the text that follows, only scratches the surface of the facts he gave us.

Limahuli is located in the *ahupua'a* (land division) of Ha'ena on the northwest coast of Kaua'i. The ancient Hawaiian ahupua'a system was created so that each division of land would be self sufficient. The ahupua'a of Ha'ena was a classic example, for it included all of the resources found in Limahuli (eg., the stream, the fertile soil, the plants and animals) as well as the marine resources of the off-shore reefs and deep sea fishing rights.

Mr. Wichman told us that people often ask him, "what is the meaning of Limahuli?" An interpretation that was given to him by a native-speaking *kupuna* (elder) is "turning hands", and refers to the hands of the *maka'āinana* or common people who lived and worked in Limahuli Valley. It was their hands that over hundreds of years, turned and cultivated the soil for their crops and turned thousands of rocks while making the countless stone *lo'i* terraces that still exist today in this valley. It was the "turning hands" of the maka'āinana that searched daily among the rocks in the stream for the *iwi* (shellfish), the *ōpae* (shrimp) and the *o'opu* (endemic fresh water fish).

The large number of ancient *lo'i ai*, or agricultural terraces (literally food terraces) in Limahuli indicate that the valley was densely populated, as was all of Hawaii before the arrival of foreign diseases. There are still remnants of the crops the ancient Hawaiian's cultivated, such as *kalo* or *taro*, banana, *'awa* (used to make an intoxicating beverage), *olonā* (used for cordage), *māmaki* (used for making *tapa* cloth) and *ōlena* (used for medicine and spices).

Habitation of the valley is thought to have started approximately 1,000 years ago and, through the practice of *mālama'aina* (caring for the land as if it was a child), the essential natural resources of the valley were never exhausted or polluted. The ancient Hawaiians carefully rotated their crops and allowed the lo'i ai to lie fallow while enriching them with organic matter. Their *kapu* system enforced a strict code of conservation by limiting the times and amounts of natural resources that could be harvested within the ahupua'a. It also addressed their pollution of the stream, ocean and earth, and the penalty for breaking a kapu, in severe cases, was death. Although it was a strict, well-enforced system, it allowed the ancient Hawaiians to live on these islands, islands that contained a limited amount of natural resources, for over 1,000 years. (Continued on page 7)

At the entrance of the Limahuli Garden, ancient terraces have been re-cultivated, as they were over 1,000 years ago (above). The Ō'hi'a lehu (Metrosideros polymorpha) is commonly known as the rain flower and is one of the native plants of the island. Its flowers can be red, salmon or yellow (left).

Legend tells us that the Menehune people were some of the original inhabitants of the valley, and that they left en masse to avoid contamination of their blood-line by later arrivals. Today, there is the same kind of concern for preserving the integrity of Limahuli's plant life. When the island of Kaua'i was first formed, a new plant arrived about every 70,000 years. With the arrival of the white man, the native ecosystems were dealt a near-fatal blow by the introduction of herbivores and alien plants (not native to Hawaii).

Between 1778 and 1800, cattle, goats and sheep (herbivores) were introduced to Hawaii. Because these new animal introductions were valuable sources of meat, they were protected and encouraged to multiply. The cattle even gained protection under a royal kapu, and eventually they proliferated to the point that large herds roamed the islands severely damaging the native forests. In addition to the immense damage done by the cattle, the goats and sheep ate the native plants in many steep rocky areas that were inaccessible to the cattle.

A few alien plants were first introduced by the ancient Hawaiian, but after the coming of the white man, the alien plants began arriving in ever-increasing numbers. Today, botanists estimate that over 4,600 alien plant species have been brought to Hawaii in the last 200 years. This compares with the 280 plants that nature brought to Hawaii over 5.5 million years. Today, man has completely altered the balance of nature, and many hundreds of these alien plant species have become naturalized and are occupying an ever-increasing percentage of Hawaii's many ecosystems.

The end result is that today, scientists have only remnants of Hawaii's unique biota left to study. It is the goal of the Limahuli Gardens and Preserve to protect and preserve the last vestiges of Hawaii's natural history, and to educate the public about their importance.

The modern history of this area shows a real lack of proper management. After the Great *Māhele* (division of land) of 1848, the Limahuli Valley became the property of an absentee landlord from Oahu, who had no real *aloha* (love) for either Kaua'i or in particular, Limahuli Valley. During this period it had no designated use and was used primarily to graze wild cattle belonging to the inhabitants of the Ha'ena area. This was a very destructive time for Limahuli Valley. Not only were the native ecosystems greatly degraded, but also a vast number of archaeological sites were severely damaged by these large clumsy animals.

In 1955, at the request of the Ha'ena Hui (the Ha'ena Hui had bought the ahupua'a of Ha'ena in 1875), the fifth circuit court of Hawaii began partition proceedings on the land. It was a difficult process and took 12 years, or until 1967, to complete. During the process, the court recognized the desire of Mrs. Juliet Rice-Wichman to see the valley preserved and, thus, assigned her 1,005 acres of Limahuli Valley. Mrs. Wichman, a *kama'āina* of Kaua'i (native born), moved to Ha'ena in 1946 and immediately recognized the need to preserve and protect Limahuli Valley. In 1967, following her wishes, the cows were removed and the valley was fenced in. From 1967 to 1971, a garden was developed and roads were put in. In 1971, the project was put on hold because of Mrs. Wichman's involvement with the establishment of the Kaua'i museum. During the hiatus, invasive alien plants took over the areas that had previously been denuded by the wild cattle. In 1976, Mrs. Wichman decided the future of the valley. She wanted to preserve the native plants and the pristine stream for future generations.

At this time, 15 acres at the mouth of the Limahuli Valley were donated to the National Tropical Botanical Gardens. The remaining 990 acres she gave to her grandson, Charles Wichman, Jr. (Continued on page 11)

View of the garden looking north to the ocean. This part of the garden has been cleared (above).
Much of the garden though, is still overgrown (left).

This large old spindly hala tree, commonly known as the screw pine (Pandanus tectorius) is seen in abundance through out the valley.

This hanging infloresence Heliconia (Heliconia rostrata) is a favorite ornamental plant in Hawaii.

After having served his apprenticeship at NTBG in Lawai, and having earned a degree in tropical horticulture from the University of Hawaii, he took over as superintendent-horticulturist of the Limahuli Gardens. Although Charles Wichman is the owner of most of the Limahuli Valley, he considers himself more the steward of the land. The original inhabitants of the valley believed that the gods owned the land and they were merely the caretakers. The concept of ownership was as foreign to them, as it is to Mr. Wichman.

Presently, Limahuli Valley is not open to the general public, although NTBG is currently asking the State for permission to operate a visitors program in the valley. Until the State grants approval of this program, the Limahuli Gardens may be visited only by members of the NTBG. (Membership information is available from the N.T.B.G., P.O. Box 340, Lawai, Kaua'i, HI 96765 or Limahuli Gardens, P.O. Box 808, Hanalei, Kaua'i, HI, 96714.) In addition to visitation by members, the garden is also used as a living classroom for students, who are brought on tours.

NTBG is currently developing a master plan for the gardens and the valley. Its main goal will be to preserve and protect the native plants and especially those on the endangered list. The 'ōhi'a lehua tree is one of the native trees being preserved, and its flowers can be red, salmon or yellow. There are examples of all three in the Limahuli Gardens. Examples of other endemic species currently being preserved or planted in the gardens are: pinwheel gardenias (Gardenia remyi and Gardenia brighamii), various species of hibiscus and the majestic koa trees which the Hawaiians brought with them and/or utilized after finding them here in Hawaii. A few examples of these plants are the kalo or taro (Colocasia esculenta), the banana (Musa troglodytarum), the hala (Pandanus tectorius), the hau (Hibiscus tilliaceus), and the kukui (Aleurities moluccana). The front part of the garden is dedicated to growing tropical plants of beauty like gingers, heliconias and other ornamental plants adapted to Limahuli's environment.

The valley is a natural treasure house of native plant materials, and during a recent survey of the flora conducted by NTBG, sixteen types of plants which exist nowhere else in the world were identified. The very nature of the valley's shape and isolation is perhaps partly responsible for this situation. These plants have developed over thousands of millions of years isolated in the bottom of Limahuli Valley by the precipitous valley walls that rise to some 2,000 feet. These plant species have developed in two botanical ecosystems: the "Lowland Rainforest" and the "Mixed Mesophytic Forest." These two ecosystems were the original homes of 70% of Kaua'i's endangered plant species and 59% of the state's. It is therefore extremely important that these areas be preserved.

In addition to these valuable plant resources, Limahuli also contains one of the few easily accessible pristine streams on Kaua'i, with many of the native fish and crustaceans still living in it. In the back of the valley there is a magnificent waterfall which drops 1,000 feet to feed the stream. The area above the waterfall, is almost inaccessible, and when research work needs to be done in this area, scientists are flown in by helicopter. It was this area of the valley that was used by the ancient Hawaiian's to collect colorful feathers from the native birds to make the intricate feather cloaks and helmets for the ali'i. The feather cloaks required thousands of feathers, and the collectors developed an interesting technique for getting them. (Continued on page 16)

The splendid Bird of Paradise (Strelitzia reginae) is also a favorite flower of the islands.

The Pāpala Kepau tree contains a gummy substance which was used by feather hunters to trap the birds.

The yellow strawberry guava trees (Psidium cattleianum f. lucidum) are alien trees that pose a serious threat to the native ecosystems in Hawaii.

The magnificent Limahuli
waterfall drops 1,000 feet
to the valley floor, feeding
the pristine stream.

The Koa (Acacia kauaiensis)
is endemic to Hawaii. These
trees are what the ancient
Hawaiians used to carve their
canoes out of.

Sunset at Makana Point illuminates an ancient agricultural altar which was used by the Hawaiians to ensure a bountiful harvest.

This Kokio hauheleula (Kokia kauaiensis) is one of the rarest endemic trees in Hawaii today.

Legend of Pōhaku-o-Kāne

The *pāpala kepau* tree contains a gummy substance which is very sticky. The hunters would put this gum on the end of a stick, and attach a flower to it,which attracted the birds. The stick was then put in a tree, and when the bird alighted on it, the gum would trap it. The birds' feathers were then plucked and the birds released. In theory the feathers were to be taken without killing the birds. In order not to have to return to the village for food, the feather hunters planted kalo and bananas in natural drainages. Remnants of these plants still exist in this area even after 200 years.

It is not known what archaeological treasures the valley may yield since very little archaeological survey work has been done and no excavations have taken place, except in the coastal sand dunes fronting the valley. In several locations in the garden, there are huge rocks, which were obviously placed there for a specific purpose. One such rock is believed to have been an agricultural altar. It was believed that by offering taro to the gods the harvest would be made more bountiful. The valley is undoubtedly an archaeological treasure house, as well as a botanical one.

It is difficult to describe Limahuli, for not only is it a place of infinite beauty, but it has a certain mystical quality. According to Mr. Wichman, Limahuli is full of *"mana"* (supernatural, or divine power) which can be felt by those in close communion with nature. Mystics from all over the world have visited Limahuli and affirmed its power. One mystic attributed it to the two huge mountains at either side of its entrance, *Pōhaku-o-Kāne* and *Makana*. Makana, is famous as the peak from which firebrands were hurled out over the ocean and viewed from both Limahuli and Kēʻē. Pōhaku-o-Kāne has a legend concerning the large stone perched near its summit. In the early times before man, rocks had life, and three rocks, two brothers and a sister decided to journey to Kauaʻi. Leaving the ocean, the sister, *Oʻo-aʻa* decided to stay on the reef and fell asleep in the warm sun. Reaching the sand dune, one of the brothers, *Pōhakuloa* decided this was the place for him, and he fell asleep. The third brother decided he wanted to climb the tall mountain, so that he could watch everything that went on. Every time he tried to reach the top, he would fall back down, breaking off pieces of himself. He caused so much commotion that the great god, *Kāne*, came to him and asked him what he was doing: He told Kāne his reasons, and Kāne said that he would get up there and fall asleep like his brother and sister. He promised Kāne he wouldn't, and so Kāne lifted him to the summit, and in return he would watch over everything and report to Kāne. According to the legend, if the rock ever falls from the mountain, the world will end.

At the end of our tour, we all felt overwhelmed by the magnitude of NTBG's and Mr. Wichman's project in Limahuli Valley, and relieved that there are people who care so much about the natural and cultural history of Hawaii. We lingered in the garden enjoying its beauty and tried to imagine how it must have been hundreds of years ago.

The following day we planned to visit the heiau at Kēʻē and survey the Kalalau trailhead there.

K Ē ʻĒ

Arriving at Kēʻē we parked our car at the end of highway 560, and decided to look at the trail ahead. We were planning a hike to Hanakāpiʻai the following day, and we wanted to see what we were up against.

The Kalalau trail was carved out by ancient Hawaiians, and was used for travel and trading in the winter, when storms and high surf precluded the use of boats and canoes. To the left of the trailhead, there was a partly overgrown stone platform, which was believed to have been the house site of *Lohiau*, a prominent chief of Kauaʻi. Legend tells us that Lohiau was the lover of the goddess *Pele*, and one of Pele's sisters danced the *hula* for Lohiau.

At the beginning of the trail, there is a little hut with visitor information, and a map of the trail. There are pictures and text describing the trail, and warning of its dangers.

Kēʻē means "avoidance" and it was perhaps given this name because of the *heiau* (ancient place of worship), which is located just above the beach. If anyone disturbed a ritual at the heiau, it was punishable by death. Kēʻē's *Ka ulu a Paoa* ("the protection of Paoa.") heiau was of great importance. *Paoa* was a famous hula master, and his *hālau hula* (hula school) was located at the back of the heiau. There was a platform and a long house in which the hula was performed, but all that remains today is the platform. The Hawaiians had no written language prior to their contact with the missionaries, so the hula and the accompanying *"meles"* (chants) not only told of the heroes and great events, but kept track of genealogies, and history.

The men and women who came to Kēʻē to study the hula, were the cream of the crop. Strict *kapu* were enforced during training. If a pupil knowingly changed a step in a hula, it was punishable by death since they were changing history.

To get to the heiau, you have to walk out on to the lava rocks on the beach, and then head inland. A heiau was, and still is, a very sacred place to most of the Hawaiian people (prior to 1778, all of the people). It gained its sacredness from the *"mana"* that was contained (or existed) in that location. Today all that remains of the heiau are several terraces of black lava rock, and the hula platform. The view from the heiau of Kēʻē beach is spectacular. There is a cathedral-like silence among the ruins, disturbed only by the surf pounding on the rocks below. From a boat off Kēʻē beach you can see the entire heiau, and it is only then that you grasp the magnitude of the construction.

Although the ancient religion was supposedly abandoned after King *Kamehameha's* death in 1819, offerings are still made to this day. It is asked that all visitors to the heiau respect the offerings and leave things undisturbed. "Pray first to the gods of your forefathers. They were here first." [1]

Just above the beach there is the Allerton House, which was used in the television mini series "The Thornbirds," a saga of Western Australia. The house marks the beginning of the Nā Pali state park, and is close to the trail. After our visit to Kēʻē, we thought we were ready to take the challenge of the Kalalau trail. Next stop Hanakāpiʻai.

Kēʻē Beach from the air, where you can see the beautiful reef which has become a popular snorkeling place (above). Looking out over the heiau to the cliffs below, there is a cathedral-like silence disturbed only by the waves crashing against the black lava rocks below (left). On the previous page, wreaths have been left as offerings to the gods.

HANAKĀPĪ'AI

They say that the hike from Kē'ē to Hanakāpī'ai is a steep mile up and a steep mile down, and when you have a lot of equipment, it seems steeper. The trail is quite narrow in places, and goes through a small waterfall at the beginning. It twists and turns and climbs, but the views of the Pali are breathtaking, and the trail is shaded by giant *kukui* trees. When you don't think you can lug the equipment any further, you finally start the descent into Hanakāpī'ai.

Hanakāpī'ai, "Bay of Sprinkling Food," is one of the places on the Nā Pali coast where camping is allowed, but permits are required. The beach only exists in the summer since the harsh winter surfs scour the coastline and leave only boulders. The beach at Hanakāpī'ai is one of the few low spots on the Kalalau trail, and from there the hike to the falls is very steep. There are two ways to see the falls; either on foot or by helicopter.

Hiking to the falls is strenuous and a lot of caution must be used, for the trail is very narrow in places. The valley contains some gigantic mango trees and one near the abandoned coffee mill is more than twenty feet in diameter. Once at the falls, a swim is a must! Swimming in the splash pool can be dangerous though, because of falling rocks. Other pools are less dangerous and equally refreshing. The scenery is superb with the falls framed in dense vegetation, making the hike well worth the effort.

By helicopter, the thrills are abundant as you hover next to the falls and sense the raw power of the water as it falls hundreds of feet to the pools below.

Hiking from Hanakāpī'ai Beach, the next point of interest is Ho'olulu, and this for us was probably the most strenuous hike.

Hanakāpī'ai Beach only exists in the summer, since the harsh winter surfs scour the coastline (opposite page).
At Hanakāpī'ai Falls, the raging waters plummet to the pools below (right).

A helicopter view of Nā Pali's highest point, the crestline is approximately 4,000 feet and to the left is the 800 foot rock face at Ho'olulu.

As we go closer you can see the overwhelming height of the cliff at Ho'olulu. From the boat as you look up there is unmistakably a feeling of ,"Oh, Wow"!!!

HO'OLULU

Just past Hanakāpī'ai, the Kalalau trail gets really steep. It climbs 800 feet in a series of switchbacks. Half way up the grade, we were all ready to throw the equipment into the ocean. Jay Schwartz, our tour boat captain had warned us about this section of the trail. He called it "Heartbreak Ridge," and said this was where people asked themselves why they had brought all that extra equipment. At the highest point, you can look way down into a sheltered bay, known as Ho'olulu, "protected water."

Ho'olulu was formed by the continuous pounding of the surf on the cliffs. The cliffs were first undermined, forming sea caves, and then the ceilings of the caves collapsed, resulting in the loss of some of the cliff. The Nā Pali coast is characterized by its many sea caves, and it is one of the fastest eroding coastlines in the world.

Ho'olulu was used as a resting place by the ancient Hawaiians for their outrigger canoes as they made their way up and down the coast. It was one of the few places that afforded this luxury.

Today, boat captains pull into Ho'olulu, not so much for the shelter, but for the overwhelming dimensions of the place. Looking up from a boat at the cliff above, is comparable to looking at the top of an eighty story building. Looking down from the Kalalau trail at a boat on the water, makes the boat look like a toy. Whether the view is from within Ho'olulu or from above, the effect is the same, breathtaking! Jay also has a name for this place, and he came up with it when he looked down into Ho'olulu from the trail, "Oh Wow!!!" Of the many sea caves in this area, the most popular one is just beyond Ho'olulu at Waiahuakua.

Hiking from Ho'olulu to Waiahuakua, you climb down into Ho'olulu Valley, which is very shady and then up the opposite side. You reach Waiahuakua when you see the 4 1/4 mile marker.

Fresh water falls through the ceiling of the two door cave from the Waiahuaka stream. This is a popular spot with the local boat captains, who rush in one door and out the other.

WAIAHUAKUA

Once you arrive in Waiahuakua Valley, you see an abundance of mango, guava and mountain apples. The vegetation is dense, and so it is a very shady place. It is not possible to see the caves from the trail, so we did this on another outing.

To see the sea caves, you must take a boat tour, and these originate from Hanalei, Tunnels Beach and Port Allen. We embarked at Hanalei, and after seeing the Limahuli Valley, Kēʻē and Hanakāpīʻai we arrived at Waiahuakua.

The two door sea cave at Waiahuakua is one of the most popular spots with tour boat captains. As we accelerated into the darkness of one door, none of us knew what to expect, and our hearts were all pounding. We all asked ourselves if this guy really knew what he was doing, and thought about that waiver we had all signed back at the dock! Then we made a quick turn past the waterfall and out through a second door into daylight, what a thrill!

Inside the cave, the waterfall, tumbling through the roof is the last forty feet of the Waiahuakua stream. The stream has gradually eroded the roof of the cave, and in the future could possibly create another open ceiling cave.

Legend tells of a fisherman who escaped from robbers because of his knowledge of the cave's other exit. The robbers waited outside the first door, while he made his escape through the other.

Waiahuakua's Valley is fairly typical of the hanging valleys along the coast, its valley floor being way above sea level. It is located five miles from Kēʻē on the Kalalau trail, and the remains of terracing testify to its former habitation. Just beyond Waiahuakua the trail drops down to 400 feet, before climbing again to a ridge of the Hanakoa Valley.

There are may ways to see the Nā Pali, some people hike all the way to Kalalau Beach from Kēʻē, others take a boat and land at Kalalau and hike back. Because of our heavy equipment, we did things a little differently. We hiked the trail all the way to Waiahuakua, and then went back to Kēʻē. We then took a boat down to Kalalau and landed on the beach there. Making our base camp at Kalalau beach, we hiked the rest of the trail to Hanakoa in a long round trip. One of our fellow campers at Kalalau commented that this was a different way to do it, and he was right, but we certainly had some memorable experiences doing it this way. So on to Kalalau...

The pirates cave is just past the two door cave along the coast. We were able to go deep into the cave and anchor for a short period of time.

KALALAU BEACH

One of the biggest thrills is to ride the waves onto Kalalau Beach.

There are only two ways you can get to Kalalau Beach, either hike the eleven miles on the Kalalau trail, or take a tour boat. There is only one company which has a permit to land at Kalalau beach, and if you opt for the latter mode of transportation, you are in for one of the biggest thrills of your life! The run down to Kalalau takes between 30 to 40 minutes from Tunnels Beach, located about fifteen minutes from Hanalei, near Kēʻē, and two zodiacs are used. The larger of the two is used for passengers, while the smaller one carries camping equipment and other essentials. The run down the coast is exhilarating in the early morning, and often the boats are accompanied by Spinner dolphin, whose name is derived from their leaping from the water and spinning in the air, while maintaining pace with the boat. The boat captains often point our places of interest along the way, even though the trip is not a tour.

Once Kalalau Beach is within sight, the larger of the two boats anchors outside the swells. Passengers are given explicit instructions on what the landing procedures will be. People are transferred to the smaller zodiac in groups of four or five, and then the fun begins. Kalalau is notorious for its high swells, so it is only possible to land a small craft. The manner in which the boat is landed takes lots of skill. Like a surfer, the boat captain must time each set of waves, and wait for a lull. When the right moment is found, the boat goes in full throttle riding the waves and surfs up the beach. At the last moment the outboard is pulled up, so as not to damage it. The sensation you get as a passenger is somewhere between an extremely fast toboggan ride, and a boogie board. After you have experienced such a landing you feel breathless, thrilled and very impressed by your boat captain's skills. Our captain was John Sargent, who was both a skillful captain and a wealth of knowledge about the Nā Pali coast.

Such landings on the beach are not only exciting for the passengers, but also for those already camping there. Landings are usually greeted by a round of resounding cheers and applause. Once on the beach, you notice several things. Nudity is common place. The noise of the surf echoes off the magnificent Pali which tower above the beach, and make you feel so small in comparison. After being overawed by your surroundings, your next task is to find a suitable place to pitch your tent.

As the tour boats travel up the coast, the Spinner dolphins enjoy a game of chase.

A lot of people camp right on the beach, but there are several draw backs to doing this. First of all, it is very hard to get your stakes to anchor in sand. Secondly, the beach becomes a furnace in the afternoon sun, and the sand becomes so hot that it burns your feet. The third, and perhaps the most convincing reason to avoid the beach, is the wind. The wind comes up in the afternoon and you can experience forty mile an hour trade winds, even in summer. There are some really good camping locations back off the beach, near the trail. Several choice spots exist near the waterfall, which is at the west end of the beach, and doubles as a communal shower. Some people prefer to camp in the caves west of the waterfall, but because of the extreme erosion in this area, it is not advisable. Just above the beach there is an open grassy area with a building just behind it, which looks as if it would be the ideal camping spot, but do not camp there, since this is an emergency helipad, which is posted as such, and is frequently used.

Camping at Kalalau Beach is regulated by permit, which can be obtained at no cost from the Department of State Parks. Camping is only permitted for five days during any one month, and permits are frequently checked by rangers. The penalty for not having a permit is a fine, and confiscation of all camping equipment. The reason for such strict regulations is that the state wishes to preserve this portion of paradise, and protect it from over use.

Kalalau Beach has many mango trees growing around the campsites, which provide shade from the hot afternoon sun. Water from the waterfall should be either boiled or treated with iodine before drinking it, and campers should be sure to have a first-aid kit, since they are 11 miles from civilization by trail, and at least 45 minutes away by boat.

*Sunrise illuminates the brooding majesty of
the Pali above Kalalau Beach.*

The sun's last golden rays strike Kalalau Beach.

Looking back along the trail towards Kalalau beach,
we headed inland into the dense valley (above).
There are many trails that can be taken to
view some of the spectacular waterfalls (left).

KALALAU VALLEY

After our thrilling experience of landing on Kalalau Beach, we made camp and headed off for the short hike up the valley. It was about 8:30 a.m. and the sun was already warming things up. We were carrying plenty of bottled water for the hike.

Coming from Kalalau Beach the trail is quite level, and passes by many campsites, which have the luxury of seclusion, but the disadvantage of distance from the nearest water source. There is a fork in the trail, which leads to a signpost indicating Ha'ena or Kalalau Valley. If you do not take the fork, you come to the site of a heiau, which has a magnificent view of both the Kalalau stream and the ocean. We took this minor detour before heading up the valley.

After returning from the *heiau*, we resumed our journey up the Kalalau Valley. The going was fairly easy to begin with, but it seemed as if we were in a jungle. There was a thick canopy of foliage overhead, until we reached "Smoke rock". All of a sudden we were out in the open, and could look back at the ocean.

Once past "Smoke rock," we re-entered thick vegetation and came upon the remains of terracing used in taro cultivation. The site was overgrown with trees and plants, and we all commented on how these terraces were highly visible from the air, but really hidden at ground level. At this point it was time to break out the mosquito repellent, since we were the main course for lunch.

As we continued, the trail got a little narrower and crossed several streams. Our objective was the twin pools at the end of the trail. As we were hiking, it was easy to imagine how *Ko'olau* the leper was able to hide in this valley. We all felt like ants crawling around in this huge valley. The fact that Kalalau means "the wanderer," probably has something to do with the sprawling nature of this valley.

After hiking for about two hours we finally reached our destination, the twin pools. The pools were about 20' x 20' and extremely refreshing. It is a good place to stop and have lunch. We took a lot of photographs, and enjoyed a swim in the pools.

Hiking back to Kalalau was a little quicker, since it was mostly downhill, but it was a lot hotter than the morning, and we consumed a lot of water by the time we reached our camp.

After resting a while, we headed west along the beach to a huge cave. The cave, Wai Honu (turtle water) is said to have been a nesting place for sea turtles. The turtles no longer lay their eggs on this coast, but the cave remains. The cave is fronted by a small sand dune, which partly obscures its entrance, and the interior of the cave has a foot or two of freshwater in it. The ceiling and interior walls of the cave serve as nesting places for shearwaters, which fly around squawking when people walk into the cave. The sand dune, in front of the cave, is a perfect spot to view one of Kalalau's famous sunsets. Watching the wild surf crash against the rockslide at the end of the beach, as the sun disappears into the ocean, is a most relaxing way to end your day.

The next day we were planning a round trip hike from Kalalau to Hanakoa Falls, and we really didn't know what we were letting ourselves in for.

As you journey along the trail, either by the beach or inland towards the valley, you can see the many colors and textures that characterize the Nā Pali coast.

Taking the trail up into the valley, you become dwarfed by the large plants, and the fluted cliffs (above). At the end of the Kalalau trail there is a refreshing pool to sit and linger by, before the journey back to camp (left).

Kalalau Valley from the lookout at Kokee Park.

*Wai Honu "turtle water" a memorable place to
sit and watch the sunset on Kalalau Beach.*

*Through the early morning mist came a solitary hiker
proceeding up "Red Hill".*

KALALAU BEACH TO HANAKOA

We left our camp at about 8 a.m. loaded down with camera equipment and water. We all thought it would be a tough hike, but our senses were not ready for what we encountered. We had all seen the trail from the ocean and had heard of how narrow it could get, but until you actually experience Kalalau trail in person, all the hearsay and reading in the world cannot describe what you see and feel.

The going was pretty easy to start, since we were familiar with the first mile or so to the signpost at the junction of the trails. We followed the sign to Ha'ena, and came to the Kalalau stream. There are ropes strung across the stream to facilitate an easy crossing. Taking off our boots we crossed to the other side. The stream was fast flowing, and the ropes were a great help. Continuing on, the trail climbed abruptly, up Ka'a'alahina ridge and brought us out on the cliff edge, giving us a wonderful view of the ocean. We were now entering the *ahapua'a* of Pōhakuao, and our next obstacle was Pu'ukula or "Red Hill," as it is known locally.

From the ocean, "Red Hill" is quite obvious, since it appears as a scar on the landscape. It is a good example of the soil erosion on the Nā Pali, caused by goats and cattle. Goats were introduced by captain Cook during his first visit, and then in the 1790's, captain George Vancouver brought more goats and some cattle, which were permitted to roam wild.

"Red Hill" did not seem so tough at the bottom, but it seemed to go on and on. Once at the top of the hill, the view of the ocean was spectacular. The trail became about ten inches wide in places and erosion caused it to disappear every now and then. Drop offs of several hundreds of feet to the ocean kept everyone alert. They say that there is a special magnetic force which keeps hikers glued to the trail, and we all knew its name, "fear." We encountered many other hardy souls along the trail, and information was always exchanged as to how far it was to Hanakoa and to Kalalau. These exchanges were always very misleading since hiking the trail east and west are two very different propositions.

Several things stuck in all of our minds as both painful and pleasurable experiences. The painful one, was the one stretch of the trail which was one continuous switchback that went up and up and up, crossing the seven valleys that make up Pōhakuao. The pleasurable ones consisted of the many streams in which we dunked our hats and poured water onto our hot heads.

There is one point where the trail follows the cliff edge, where you see a rock formation (*"Puka"*) with two large holes in it, that looks like a window. From the right location, you would be able to look through, back towards Kalalau beach. At another point you can see the sea arch at Waiku'auhoe and the waterfall plunging from the rocks above. There is still evidence of the cattle ranching which went on in this area, with the odd post and strand of barbed wire. Perhaps one of the most intriguing things about this whole hike is the constant change of terrain. You wind your way along the coast for a while, and then go inland to a valley, and this pattern continues for most of the hike. (Continued on page 40)

View of the Sea Arch at Waiku'auhoe from the Kalalau trail (above). As our helicopter comes closer to the cliffs edge, we are able to view the Sea Arch, as the stream from the valley above, flows to the ocean below (left).

The tour boats travel under the arch when weather permits and fresh water from the stream above splashes into the boats.

*A rock formation resembling the Matterhorn
in the ahupua'a (land division) of Pōhakuao.*

Some of the valleys are very shady and one valley had giant *'ape* growing. (a plant resembling the *taro*, but of gigantic proportions.) Because of the change in locales, there are noticeable temperature changes, and when all of a sudden you find yourself in the broiling sun, you reach for the water bottle more frequently.

There are parts of the trail which are like a giant serpent, and you can look across a valley and see other hikers on one of the loops, and observe the ground you have already covered. The hike to Hanakoa is a little deceptive, since you see the valley for a long time before you actually get into it. Once you enter Hanakoa, you notice two things, the vegetation is a lot denser, and it feels more humid.

We all expected to be able to see the falls from the trail, and we began to wonder if we would ever get there. Finally, we reached the marker that read 1/3 mile to the falls, and we all breathed a sigh of relief. The sign was a little misleading, since it seemed much more than a third of a mile. The going was so tough at times, that we wondered if we were on a trail. It was very steep, narrow and overgrown. Things got so bad at one point, that we sent one member of our party on ahead to see if we were going in the right direction. We all breathed a sigh of relief when he told us that the falls were just ahead. By the time we got up to the falls, it was about 1 p.m., and we were a little concerned about the time it would take us to get back to Kalalau, but this was soon forgotten when we viewed Hanakoa Falls.

The narrow walls of the horseshoe-shaped valley echoed the continuous sound of the thundering water. The water spilling from the valley rim tumbles to a huge eerie splash pool 1,000 feet below. It is a place of raw power, where people are dwarfed by the immensity of the falls and the vastness of the pool. While we were there, many helicopters darted in like dragon flies for a quick view of the falls.

As with many Hawaiian place names, there are different interpretations of "Hanakoa." It can mean "bay of the warrior," or "bay of the Koa tree." The Tahitians who migrated to Kaua'i did not have strong trees like the *koa*, so when they arrived, they named the tree "koa," which was their word for warrior, hence the two possible meanings of "Hanakoa."

From our personal experience of the valley and the trail, it is not hard to believe that this was a place where warriors trained. There is some evidence of agriculture in the form of overgrown terracing. The climate in Hanakoa would certainly have lent itself to cultivation, since it receives about 130 inches of rain per year.

The valley, today, is a popular camping place and there are many good campsites down by the stream, but the mosquito population is prolific, due to the wetness of the area, so carry plenty of repellent.

After taking a refreshing dip in the splash pool, and eating lunch, we got down to the serious business of trying to capture the magnificence of Hanakoa Falls on film. This done, we started on our return journey with a little apprehension.

The trail back to Kalalau was a lot easier, since we were very familiar with the terrain, and best of all, we got to go down the giant switchback instead of up. We made excellent time going back, and when we arrived in camp, we all had a feeling of accomplishment. Kalalau to Hanakoa Falls, round trip in one day!! We had all talked about losing weight, getting in shape and being ready for the trip, but other things always got in the way. Nevertheless, we did it, and so can you!

Back in camp, we started dinner and watched the moon rise over Nākeikianā'i'iwi and the sun set on Kalalau....

Hanakóa Valley where the vegetation is very dense and the humidity very high.

Hanakoa Falls is possibly the most spectacular on the Nā Pali Coast, cascading down 1,000 feet to a large pool below.

From our camp, we watched the moon rise above the fluted cliffs.

A peaceful sunset at Kalalau, but when the winter storms hit, you can see what can be left behind.

Nākeikianā'iwi, children of the I'iwi bird.

NĀKEIKIANĀ'I'IWI

From Kalalau beach looking inland, you see a rock formation which looks like the spires of a Gothic cathedral. This is Nākeikianā'i'iwi. (children of the i'iwi bird.) Legend tells us that a man named I'iwi, one of the last surviving members of the *Mu* people, lived in a cave far above Kalalau beach with his two children, Kua and Hiki. Most of the Mu people had left Kaua'i along with the *Menehunes*, but I'iwi stayed on, growing his bananas, and caring for his children. I'iwi's wife had turned to stone when she could no longer bear being without company of other women, and had gone out into the sunlight. The Mu people were people of the deep forest, and children of the night. They slept during daylight and worked at night.

I'iwi's two children longed to play with the children of Kalalau, and one moonlit night when they went down to trade bananas for fish, they found the children playing in the moonlight. They were so excited that they played all night long, and realized too late that the sun was rising. They hurried up the cliff, but were struck by the sun's rays and turned to stone. Their father seeing the approach of day, knew he had lost his children. When night fell, he found two rocks which were his children, and grieved for them. Having lost both his wife and children, he waited beside the rock, which had been his wife for the sun's rays.

I'iwi was said to have been a member of the Mu people, and the next valley going westward is reputed to have been their home, "the Valley of the Lost Tribe," Honopū Valley.

We had been told that on calm days people swam between Kalalau beach and Honopū, but we knew that the ocean conditions were unpredictable. Kalalau is known for its swells, and sometimes they are so bad, that boats can't get in, and campers either have to hike back eleven miles or swim out through the surf to the boat. The day we chose to leave Kalalau, this happened to us. When the announcement was made, either swim or stay, there were many faces that expressed horror. Most people had heard of the treacherous swimming conditions off Kalalau, and here was someone telling them they would have to risk it!

Swimmers went in small groups, weak swimmers being helped by the strong. This was an experience none of us will ever forget. We had to wait for a lull in the swells and run out into the surf until we could run no more. Then we swam for the boat and the adrenalin was really pumping. Once on the boat, all the moments of doubt disappeared, and we all reflected on how easy it had been, and it sure beat hiking back eleven miles!!

After leaving Kalalau, you can only see the coast by boat and helicopter. Helicopter tours are available from Lihue and Princeville, while boat tours leave from Hanalei, Port Allen and Tunnels Beach. We found the best way to see the valleys was by helicopter.

Honopū Arch is one of the most photographed landmarks on the Nā Pali coast.

HONOPŪ

Honopū, "Bay of the Conch," is possibly one of the most photographed spots on the Nā Pali coast. It's huge sea arch separates two white sand beaches. The makers of "Star Wars" were attracted to this site, and they filmed the scene where the two robots were on the sand dunes to the east of the arch. When "King Kong" was remade in 1976, Honopū was again selected and the waterfall near the arch was where Jessica Lange was seen bathing. Honopū Valley, just above the beaches, is also known as "the Valley of the Lost Tribe."

The "Lost Tribe" were perhaps the legendary *"Mu"* people, who disappeared without a trace, leaving only their name to this valley. The valley shows no evidence of cultivation, and it is thought that natives may have grown their taro in nearby Kalalau. The valley, because of its narrowness and steep sides, does not get alot of sunlight, and so would not have been an ideal cultivation spot. Access into the valley is very difficult and is discouraged because of the danger. This area is not open to the public, and special permits are required to enter the valley. We saw the whole valley from a helicopter and we will all remember hovering near the huge sea arch.

There is an eerie feeling about Honopū, which is perhaps caused by its isolation. Like Ho'olulu, the "open ceiling" cave, located just beyond Honopū and near Awa'awapuhi, offered boats and canoes a resting place on their way up the coast. We next flew into Awa'awapuhi.

Honopū beach, where the water is warm, clear and laps against the tranquil shore.

Aerial view of Honopū,"the Valley of the Lost Tribe".

Honopū Valley, where legend tells us of the ancient Mu people, who disappeared without a trace.

Aerial view of the Awa'awa'puhi Trail.

Awa'awapuhi Valley known as the "slithering eel."

AWA'AWAPUHI

Awa'awapuhi,"the valley of the slithering eel" gets its name from a legend. The natives believed that a giant eel slithered up onto the land when lava was still flowing and formed the valley. The valley is a 3,000 foot chasm that twists back inland, and is somewhat inaccessible. There are no trails leading in which are open to the public, and trying to hike down from Kokee is suicidal. From a boat, only the mouth of the valley is visible, but from the air, the "eel-like" shape is easily seen. Like Honopū, the valley is very narrow, and because of this, the valley doesn't get a lot of sunlight. This combined with the narrowness precluded any cultivation, and so limited the habitation of this valley.

Today one of the best ways to see the valley, is to go up to Koke'e Park. From Lihue, go south on route 50 and turn right on route 550, near Waimea. It is 38 miles, and will take about an hour and a half. Once there, take the Awa'awapuhi trail, which drops down 1,000 feet in a relatively short distance. The hike is well worth the effort, for the viewing is of both Awa'awapuhi and Nu'alolo valleys. It is not possible to hike all the way down, for there are sheer drop- offs that have caused the deaths of several unwary hikers.

Most helicopter tours fly over Awa'awapuhi, but we persuaded our pilot to fly inside the valley. The walls are so narrow that you feel as if the rotors will touch them. The experience was quite frightening, but the view was worth it.

Nu'alolo located just west of Awa'awapuhi is one of the richest archaeological sites on the Nā Pali coast.

As you leave Awa'awapuhi you come across another of the splendid Nā Pali caves. During the winter months the open ceiling cave becomes a large blow-hole as the waves crash against the cliffs forcing the water out.

Simply breathtaking... a view of the open ceiling cave from inside, as you look up into the beautiful afternoon summer sky.

The reef at Nu'alolo Kai, a popular snorkeling spot, where tour boats stop to enjoy the beautiful and tranquil bay .

NU 'ALOLO

We saw Nu'alolo from both boat and helicopter, and to fully appreciate this locale, we would recommend doing the same.

There are two Nu'alolo's, Nu'alolo *'Āina*, meaning of the land, and Nu'alolo *Kai*, meaning of the sea. A steep cliff separates the two, and up until the abandonment of the settlements in the early 1900's, there was a ladder connecting the two. Nu'alolo 'Āina was quite extensively cultivated, and the remains of ancient terraces can be seen to this day. Nu'alolo Kai was a fishing village, and so the two communities combined were self sufficient.

In 1958, the Emory archaeological expedition conducted a major excavation of the area. Many stone platforms tucked into the cliffs were found, and these were house sites. Over 4,000 artifacts were uncovered, some of them unique to Kaua'i. Implements used in the preparation of *poi* were quite standard throughout the Hawaiian Islands, but it was only on Kaua'i that "ring and stirrup" poi pounders have been found. This discovery at Nu'alolo was extremely important, for it helped place the origins of the island's later arrivals. Radio carbon dating has put a date of the early 12th and 13th centuries on these artifacts. Similar *poi* pounders of the "ring and stirrup" type have been found on the island of *Uahuka* in the *Marquesas*, and they date anywhere from 600 to 1300 A.D., so the origin of the later arrivals in Kaua'i can be established quite plausibly.

The location of the house sites in the lee of the cliff was the reason for the preservation of so many artifacts. Bone and shell fishhooks, adzes, sinkers, cordage, matting, and gourds were all found and preserved by the salt spray.

The cliffs around Nu'alolo were used as burial sites. Burial sites depended on rank. The *ali'i* were always buried in secret places, the bones, wrapped in *tapa* cloth, hidden in caves or niches in inaccessible cliff sites. The reason for the secrecy was the belief that the *"mana"* (power, or spirit) remained in the bones. It was a common practice to make fishhooks out of human bone, and so the necessary secrecy existed.

Ali'i were often buried with their canoes, or with prized possessions, and it is reported that some explorers found such a site in the 1920's but inadvertently dislodged the canoe, which was destroyed in its fall from the cliffs. It was considered an honor to share in the death of an ali'i, so there were many instances of ali'i going to their graves accompanied by some of their followers.

The cliffs between Nu'alolo'Āina and Nu'alolo Kai are very dangerous and should be avoided. The local tour boat captains frequent this area because there is a coral reef, which is a popular snorkeling spot. On our tour boat we stopped here and snorkeled on the reef. The multitude of brightly colored fish is spectacular, and they come to the boats when food is thrown into the water. Tour boats often turn around here since they don't include Miloli'i, the next valley along the coast in their tour. Since our tour was a charter we continued on down the coast and saw Miloli'i from the boat.

Helicopter view of one of Nā Pali's many hanging valleys.

Miloli'i is one of only three places where commercial boats can land people on the beaches. It has the best facility for camping, and is a popular spot.

Miloli'i Valley is the site of two ruined temples, surrounded by cliffs which were used extensively for ancient burial sites.

MILOLI'I

Miloli'i means "fine twist," or "swirling current." It was known for its good cordage, and legend has it that it was named after an expert sennit weaver. Sennit was a kind of rope usually made from coconut husks. Miloli'i had everything to make it self-sufficient; its reef provided fish, while its valley was cultivated for taro.

Two *heiaus* once existed at this site and it was an important community. Like Nu'alolo, the cliffs were used extensively for burial sites. In the 1870's there was a school house in the valley, but by the early 1900's most of the valley's population had either moved away or died from disease.

Today, Miloli'i is one of only three places where commercial boats can land people on the beaches. It has the best facility for camping, and is a popular spot.

The habitation of the Nā Pali coast, starting around the tenth century, ended with the abandonment of the village at Miloli'i around 1919.

Our tour also ended at Miloli'i. We hope you have enjoyed sharing our journey with us, as much as we have enjoyed sharing it with you. No matter which way you choose to see the Nā Pali coast, it will be magnificent...

Mahalo....from the production team of Unique Adventures Press

ACKNOWLEDGEMENTS

*T*here are many people and organizations we would like to thank for their assistance and contributions to this book.

Thanks to Jay Schwartz, the captain on our very first boat trip whose stories of the Nā Pali coast inspired us to start this project. We would also like to thank Jay for all his efforts on our photo shoots.

We would like to thank our writer, Graham V. Bell, who combined all of the production teams personal experiences of Nā Pali with its myths and legends.

Our thanks go to Brian McDonald, our fearless photographer, whose skill and eye brought beauty to this project.

Special thanks to Mr. Charles "Chipper" Wichman, Jr., of the Limahuli Gardens, Ha'ena, who spent so much of his valuable time and was able to express his dreams so clearly to us.

Bill Reed (helicopter pilot), thanks for the wonderful views of the island, your skill and patience.

Also thanks to:

Mr. Paul Claeghorn of the Bishop Museum for taking his valuable time to review our text.

The Kaua'i Museum

The Kaua'i Historical Society

The Hawaiian Department of Business and Economic Development

The Hawaiian Visitor's Bureau

The Division of State Parks

John Sargent, our thanks go to you for getting us off Kalalau beach safely and to all the other warm and helpful people of the island of Kaua'i.

Doug and Barbara Luhmann
Unique Adventures Press

BIBLIOGRAPHY

Edward H. Bryan, Jr., *Ancient Hawaiian Life*, Honolulu Hawaii, Advertising Publishing Company, 1938.

Kamehameha Schools, *Ancient Hawaiian Civilization*, Honolulu, 1965, (Rev. Ed.).

Patrick Vinton Kirch, *Feathered Gods and Fishooks: An Introduction to Hawaiian Archaeology and Pre-history*, Honolulu: University of Hawaii Press, © 1985.

Ross H. Cordy, *A Study of Prehistoric Social Change: The Development of Complex Societies in the Hawaiian Islands*, New York: Academic Press, © 1981.

Hawaiian Mythology, (with a new introduction by Katharine Luomala), Honolulu, University of Hawaii Press, ©1970.

D.M. Kaaiakamanu and J.K. Akina. (Translated by Akaiko Akana), *Hawaiian Herbs of Medicine Value Found Among the Mountains and Elsewhere in the Hawaiian Islands, and Known to the Hawaiians to Possess Curative and Palliative Properties Most Effective in Removing Physical Ailments*, Rutland, Va., C.E. Tuttle Co.,1972.

Vivian Laubach Thompson, *Hawaiian Tales of Heroes and Champions*, Honolulu, University of Hawaii Press, ©1971

Julius Scammon Rodman, *The Kahuna Sorcerers of Hawaii, Past and Present: With A Glossary of Ancient Religious Terms, and the Books of the Hawaiian Royal Dead*, Hicksville, N.Y., Exposition Press, © 1979.

Valerio Valeri, Translated by Paul Wissing, *Kingship and Sacrifice: Ritual and Society in Ancient Hawaii*, Chicago, University of Chicago Press, ©1985.

Helen Gay Pratt, *The Hawaiians, an Island People*, Rutland, VT., C.E. Tuttle Co., © 1963.

Mary Kawena Pukui, (collected or suggested by Mary Kawena Pukui,retold by Caroline Curtis, illustrated by Richard Goings), *Tales of the Menehune, and Other Short Legends of the Hawaiian Islands*, Honolulu, Kamehameha Schools Press, 1970.

Martha Warren Beckwith, *Hawaiian Mythology* (new introduction by Katharine Luomala), Honolulu, University of Hawaii Press, 1970.

Robert Wenkam, *Kaua'i and the Park Country of Hawaii*, Sierra Club Exhibit Format Series.

Kathy Valier, *On the Nā Pali Coast, A Guide for Hikers and Boaters*, Honolulu, University of Hawaii Press, © 1988.

Mary Kawena Pukui, Samuel H. Elbert, Esther T. Mookini, *Place Names of Hawaii*, Honolulu, University of HawaiiPress, © 1966.

Edward Joesting, *Kaua'i, The Separate Kingdom*, University of Hawaii Press and Kaua'i Museum Association, Limited, 1984.

Frederick B. Wichman, *Kaua'i Tales*, Honolulu, Bamboo Ridge Press, 1985.

Magazine Articles:

Rita Ariyashi, *Hawaii's Historic Hula* (Hula Performances and Festivals), V. 169, "Travel-Holiday", June, '88, P.22 (4).

John Skow, *In Praise of the Goddess Pele: Hula Flourishes in a Hawaiian Cultural Revival*, "Time", Aug. 24, '87, P. 67(1).

Ethel A. Starbird, *Kaua'i — The Island That's Still Hawaii*, "National Geographic", November 1977.

Footnote1: (page 17) Sam Pua Haaheo, *A Kahuna who taught hula and mele over 130 years ago*, "Time", Aug. 24, '87.

GLOSSARY

Ahupua'a- Land division usually extending from the uplands to the sea.

Ali'i- Chief, king or queen, royal, chiefly, or kingly.

Ali'i Nui - Chief who was considered great.

Āina- Land, earth.

Aloha- Love, mercy, compassion, greeting to a loved one.

'Awa- The Kava (Piper methysticum).

Hala- The pandanus or screw pine.

Hālau hula- Long house, as for hula instruction.

Heiau- Pre-christian place of worship.

Hula- Song or chant expressed in dancing.

I'wi- Shellfish.

Kahuna- Priest, minister, expert in any profession.

Kālaimoku- Counselor, prime minister, to hold a high office.

Kalo- Taro, native Hawaiian vegetable.

Kāma'āina- Native born, host; native plant.

Kamehameha I- Overlord of Hawaii Island, conquered Maui, Lanai and Molokai, then defeated Oahu and later by treaty, Kaua'i would be added to his kingdom.

Kāne-Name of one of the four leading Hawaiian Gods.

Kapu- Taboo, law, special forbidden taboos.

Kaula- Rope, cord, string, or line.

Kauwā- Untouchable, outcast, pariah.

Koa- An endemic forest tree, the largest and most valued of the native trees. Its fine wood was used, for canoes and surfboards.

Konohiki- Headman of an ahupua'a land division under the chief.

Kukui- Candlenut tree, the state tree.

Lohiau- One of the great chiefs of Kaua'i.

Lo'i- Irrigated terrace, especially for taro, but also for rice.

Lo'i ai- Growing of taro for food.

Māhele- Portion, division, department or land division.

Maka'āinana- Commoner, people in general.

Makana- Gift or present, (Makana Pt. was where the firebands, were displayed as gifts to the gods).

Mālama'āina- To take care of the land

Māmaki- A small native tree whose bark is very coarse.

Mana- Supernatural or divine power.

Manahune- Name the Tahitians called themselves of small physical stature.

Marquesas- The northernmost islands of French Polynesia, in the South Pacific.

Mele- Song, chant of any kind, poems.

Menehune- Legendary race of small people who worked at night building fishponds and roads.

Mu- Legendary people of Kaua'i.

O'o-a'a- Legendary sister of Pohaku-o-Kane.

Ōhi'alehua- The tree Metrosideros collina

Ōlena- Turmeric, a kind of ginger; used medicinally and as a source of dye.

Olonā- A native shrub; the very strong.

O'opu- General name for fishes included in the families Eleotridae and Gobiidae; some live in salt water near the shore, others in fresh water.

Ōpae- General name for shrimps and prawns.

Pāpala kēpau- Species of small shrubs and trees with a gum substance.

Pele- In Polynesian mythology, the goddess of fire and volcanoes, espcially in Hawaii and Tahiti.

Pōhakuloa - Legendary brother of Pohaku-o-Kane.

Pōhaku-o-Kāne- Legendary male stone.

Poi- The Hawaiian staff of life, made from cooked taro corms, pounded until smoothed and thinned with water.

Raiatea- A south pacific island in French Polynesia and the largest of the Leeward group of the Society Islands.

Uahuka- Small island of the Marquesas Islands in the South Pacific Ocean.